The PSYCHOLOGY of Staying Rich

The PSYCHOLOGY *of*
Staying Rich

HOW TO PRESERVE WEALTH AND ESTABLISH AN ENDURING FINANCIAL LEGACY

J. TED OAKLEY

RIVER GROVE
BOOKS

Published by River Grove Books
Austin, TX
www.rivergrovebooks.com

Distributed by River Grove Books

Design and composition by Oxbow Advisors
Cover design by Oxbow Advisors

Publisher's Cataloging-in-Publication data is available.

Print ISBN: 978-1-63299-311-3

eBook ISBN: 978-1-63299-312-0

Second Edition

Are you confident your investments will
make your wealth last a lifetime?

Do you wonder how you can
keep the family fortune in the family?

Have you recently sold a business?
Feeling more worried than triumphant?

Are you struggling to find sound
and trustworthy investment advising?

Are you inundated with Wall Street
investment groups trying to sell you with
the same booklets, the same graphs,
the same pictures, and the same people?

◑

Oxbow Advisors

At OXBOW ADVISORS, we're not Wall Street. We are an Austin, Texas–based wealth management company specializing in the needs of families with significant wealth—many of them just this side of liquidity events such as selling a business or inheriting assets.

Unlike many of the investment firms at your door, we're not paid to sell you any product, any portfolio, anything. Instead, as independent advisors, we assess all options in search of the best quality investments to fit your needs.

What we do is simple, but hard to find in today's investment world: We protect the wealth you've worked hard to create. You tell us what you need to achieve financially—for yourself and for your family—and our job is to help you get there.

Oxbow Advisors
Oxbowadvisors.com
512-386-1088

CONTENTS

PART THREE

Next-Generation Failure—And How to Avoid It

Introduction

Getting rich and staying rich are two totally different challenges. Strange as it may sound, holding on to wealth often turns out to be harder than getting it in the first place. In my 40 years of watching families' fortunes rise and fall, I've observed good, bad, and ugly methods, behaviors, and outcomes. I've also seen many of the same mistakes made over and over, family after family, generation after generation. Approximately 65% of *Forbes* billionaires are first generation. Twenty percent are second generation and a paltry 10% third generation. Three percent make it to the fourth generation and only 1% to the fifth. Why is that? Where does the money go?

There have been plenty of books written about how to get rich, but very few on how to stay that way. As an entrepreneur and business owner, you know how to make money and control your situation. But if you're selling or otherwise making a big change in your financial status, you need to know that the mindset you needed to achieve wealth is not the same as the one you need to protect it. This is not the time to be confident; it's a time to focus on learning, on humility, and on family. If you want to hang on to your wealth throughout your lifetime, and especially if you want to pass it on to future generations, this wide-open book about the psychology of staying rich will start you down the right road. We'll talk about outside influences, inside influences, and the psychological miscues that can trip up even smart, successful people. We'll look at the biggest pitfalls to staying rich and the common traits of the people who make it happen.

If this book applies to you, congratulations on making your fortune. Here at Oxbow Advisors, we understand the hard work, commitment, smarts, and sacrifice it took to get where you are today. You're on top of the world right now, but as you move on to the next phase of wealth—figuring out how to keep it and keep it in the family—the odds are against you again. You're following in the footsteps of individuals and families throughout history, the majority of whom managed to lose their money almost as fast as they made it. It doesn't have to be that way. The sooner you start changing your focus from the psychology of *getting* rich to the psychology of *staying* rich, the better.

PART ONE

The Problem of Wealth Loss

CHAPTER 1

What is "Rich"?

Wealth is always a question of relevance. For those among the 70% of lower-income individuals who will stay that way throughout their lives, having a million dollars might be "rich." For the 59% who live paycheck to paycheck, even a lesser sum might qualify. A recent study by Charles Schwab Bank says that $2.4 million is the net worth benchmark for rich—a figure 30 times the US average of $80,000.

From our vantage at Oxbow, there are many ways to define rich, but we use the benchmark of accumulated wealth over $20 million. It's an ultra-high figure, but we see all the time that there's no number investors agree is enough. What matters more than any number is whether the wealth meets these two criteria:

1. It's enough money that you will never run out.

2. It's enough that if you ceased to earn or invest right now you'd still be set for life.

The basics of this book revolve around what it takes to maintain this level of wealth (and why so many people can't seem to do it). Over the years at Oxbow, we have developed a deep understanding of what rich is. We've also determined the number one ingredient to staying rich, which we will discuss in later chapters. Seventy-five percent of the truly rich grew up poor or middle class. Eighty-five percent are married. Almost all of them attribute their wealth to hard work and personal ambition. A low percentage inherited their wealth, but those who hang on to it know they need to work hard to keep it.

In our experience, many among the rich are never satisfied with their level of wealth. If they have $10 million, they want $20 million. If they have $30 million, they want $50 million, and at $50 million they want $100 million. Is that part of the psychology of staying rich? Here at Oxbow, we find that the endless chasing is part of the problem, not part of the solution. Everyone wants solid investments with steady returns, but there comes a time when the wealthy need to change focus from throwing money after the next big thing to hanging on to what they have and ensuring its longevity. That's the first step in the psychology of staying rich.

OXBOW NOTE

If you are a first-generation wealth earner who's just sold your company, this is a critical time in your financial life and an area of specialization for us at Oxbow Advisors. For free copies of more of our books about this make-or-break time, contact us at OxbowAdvisors.com.

CHAPTER 2

Don't Let Yourself Be on This List

Before we dig deep into the psychology of staying rich, let's look at some spectacular examples of what not to do.

It's easy to think that once you've made your fortune, you and yours are set for life, but the list of individuals and families who've had wealth and lost it throughout history is too long to write. We see it in the headlines, the stories of people ranging from John Wayne to Mike Tyson, Michael Jackson to Larry King, Mark Twain to MC Hammer to Johnny Depp. Lisa Marie Presley, who inherited $100 million in 1993, declared in a lawsuit 25 years later that she was down to her last $14,000 due to poor financial guidance. John McAfee, who made $100 million with his software company, lost 96% of that wealth in a decade or so of frivolous spending and bad investments. It happens to people with every kind of success, from every kind of family, and in every kind of industry. It happens to business owners, heirs, movie stars, athletes, writers, doctors, lawyers, inventors, investors, and lottery winners. It happens to savvy businesspeople who struggled and sacrificed to build their wealth, and it happens to people who got rich in a windfall. At Oxbow, we see the trend of wealth loss played out up close and personal, often in the form of inexperienced, risk-loving, and maverick investors who refuse to listen to reason and solid investment sense. Over the past 40 years we've learned that the size of the wealth simply does not matter—any fortune that can be made can be lost. We've seen personal wealth ranging from $5 million to $200 million go down the drain.

If you're new to wealth or on the outside looking in, it can seem inconceivable that a person could amass enough money to last a lifetime—or several lifetimes—only to let it slip away, but that's exactly what happens, time and again. It seems that where there's a way to get rich, there's a way to lose it all. Those losses cause terrible sorrow and pain to those who once had everything. Many spend the rest of their lives regretting the decisions that caused their financial downfall. When I see families heading down this road, squandering their wealth, I'm always a little sick about it, because it doesn't have to happen.

CAUTIONARY TALE

One of the best illustrations of getting rich and losing everything is the story of legendary stock trader Jesse Livermore. It's going on a hundred years since Livermore's spectacular rise and fall, but we still talk about him in the investment world as the ultimate cautionary tale. Livermore was a brilliant man who made and lost many fortunes in his life, but his greatest coup came on the worst day in stock market history. When Black Tuesday hit in 1929, Livermore wasn't among the traders who were wiped out. Sensing unease in the market, he shorted it. As the financial world crashed down around him, Livermore made the equivalent of $3 billion in today's dollars.

That should be the end of the story—*Man Shorts Market During Historic Crash; Makes Fortune*—but that's not why we remember Livermore. Even in an era when the reality of risk was in headlines across the country, Livermore managed to lose it all—$100 million Depression-era dollars—in five years. By 1934, he was in the midst of his third bankruptcy (and his second divorce). In 1940, broken and broke, he took his own life.

A FAMILY'S TOTAL LOSS

Wealthy families are impacted as bluntly as individuals. In Frances Stroh's book, *Beer Money*, she recounts the days of being ultra-wealthy in Grosse Pointe, Michigan. The Stroh family's wealth at its pinnacle in the 1980s was estimated by *Forbes* to be about $9 billion in today's dollars. Today the money is almost completely gone. What went wrong? How can a family lose a fortune of that magnitude? For starters, too many buyouts and acquisitions put their great American brewery in debt. The debt slowed their response to a market that started wanting lite beer. Bad investments in real estate and biotech kept the losses coming, and all the while more heirs demanded dividends. It may sound like a story of uniquely bad breaks, but the fact is the Strohs' experience is typical of how a family's wealth disintegrates.

AN AMERICAN LEGEND

Let's talk about one more family, one of the most famous in American history. Cornelius Vanderbilt was the richest man in the country at the time of his death in 1877, with a fortune that would be worth more than $2 billion today. It's ironic and prophetic that the tycoon once said, "Any fool can make a fortune. It takes a man of brains to hold on to it after it's made."

Just 30 years after Vanderbilt's death, not one member of his family was among the wealthiest Americans. Worse, Vanderbilt's descendants came to nothing but trouble with their money. His son considered it his burden and the source of his unhappiness. His grandson once said inherited wealth was "as certain a death to ambition as cocaine is to morality."

Rather than finding security in their wealth, the family was miserable and wasted it away.

You hear about the Vanderbilt story when people talk about lost wealth, but you don't hear about the thousands of individuals and families who lose smaller, more personal fortunes every year. They're people who worked hard and sacrificed and built something that had tremendous value, often from nothing. They're people who've made $10 or $25 or $100 or $500 million, not overnight, but over decades. Most of those fortunes are soon lost to bad investments, market changes, wild spending, family squabbles, shady advisors, and other equally ugly fates. How do you protect against those things? There's no way to create a plan that specifically blocks against each. What there is, though, is a mindset and a commitment—the psychology of staying rich. If you're thinking about it and guarding at the outset, you can be ahead of the game.

In my four decades of dealing with other people's wealth, I've seen large estates blown up time and again. I always wish I could counsel these families before they go over the waterfall, but unfortunately many of them are not ready to listen until it's too late.

OXBOW NOTE

In my book $20 Million and Broke, *I outline the reasons wealth loss is so common in detail and with real-life examples. If you'd like a complimentary copy of this book or any of my other titles, contact us at OxbowAdvisors.com.*

CHAPTER 3

The Nature of Wealth

The nature of a family's wealth is a major factor in its ability to keep the money moving from generation to generation. One of the biggest distinctions in how this happens (or doesn't) is whether the business is still going or has been sold.

When families have a business, they have a center to rally around. When the business is a brand, they tend to stay together and pull together. For example, if a family owns a branded beer distributor (like Miller or Budweiser) or a food company (like Mars Candy), the brand and everything associated with it is passed down through generations. Gen-2 and Gen-3 grow up in the business and it becomes a part of their identity, so it's not just Dad's or Grandpa's business, but the whole family's golden egg. Brands become disciplines and habits, part of the psyche of the family that pulls the offspring together. Having a strong brand is one of the surest ways to successfully hang on to wealth and push it to the second generation.

Even if the business doesn't have the kind of strong identity that comes with a household name, it's still possible to rely on it as the center for a family's wealth continuity. This requires making an effort to ensure the kids and grandkids identify with the company and the work that's done there, so they recognize it as an interest in their own lives. Of course the problem with businesses and brands is that they don't last forever. Businesses grow and change. Many families eventually sell and convert to cash. That is the moment when families experience a giant shift: A shared brand is a cohesive force, but liquid cash tends to pull people apart. When the company that acted as a magnet pulling everyone together doesn't exist anymore, it's easy for both the family and the money to scatter.

At Oxbow, we consistently find that families with tremendous liquid wealth do better when they invest together than apart. It makes sense. After all, a $100 million investor will see more deals and opportunities than five separate $20 million investors.

When the money isn't tied together, any number of forces can pull the family apart. Sometimes a spouse who married in says, "Let's build something of our own and not be tied to your parents and siblings all the time." Sometimes one sibling accuses another, maybe one with a more prominent role in the business, of demanding too big a share. Individuals look to move out of the shadow of the family. And then there are the inevitable temptations of the wealth itself—like extravagant spending and consumption—that always lead to wealth being diluted.

THE BRAND-LESS FORTUNE

So if you don't have a family brand, are you doomed to lose your wealth? Not necessarily. We can learn a lot from the culture of brand-based wealth, even when the brand itself is a thing of the past. When the brand is active, things like profit and loss statements, shareholders' meetings, and jobs in the business keep the family engaged.

After the sale, all that evaporates and what's left is just a bunch of money.

The brand worked well to pull the family together because it provided both a culture and cohesive habits. After a business is sold, a different kind of force needs to replace it—one that creates the same kind of gentle leverage toward the family and toward wealth continuity. The logical shift is from a business brand to a family brand—something that Gen-2 and Gen-3 can strongly identify with if you do it right. The family "brand" can consist of any number of different elements, but some of the most effective are a family business board and, critically, some kind of family philanthropy. Shared wealth and shared purpose work together to create a strong sense of family identity.

These measures can't be taken in name only, and they can't be created overnight. If you're serious about preserving the "brand effect" in your family, you and your spouse will need to do the groundwork to build it and then gain full buy-in from your heirs. It's a huge logistical and emotional challenge, but it can be done.

The logistical side of the challenge is in figuring out the structure and form the official family plan will take. What will it look like? What will the family produce? How will the entity help assure long-term financial security through generations? What philanthropic interests will it support? Who will have what role in the infancy of the family organization? How will it pull everyone together? Does the plan include some kind of outside advising as a reality and honesty check on the financial side of things? All of these issues can be resolved and worked out through planning and organization—perhaps with the help of a trusted advisor to help them take shape.

The emotional challenge can be harder. It ties directly into whether family members will want to be invested in the family brand in the long and short term. In his book *Family Wealth Continuity*, author David Lanksy talks about the concept of *familyness*. In essence, this is the importance of intangible factors like family harmony, goodwill toward each other, and, of course, love. If you truly want to create generational wealth transition, familyness is a key piece. You can't make siblings or grandchildren bond and care for each other, but you can set an example of offering unconditional support, prioritizing family relationships, and bringing your family together for events that are as much about bonding and affection as they are about investment and financial legacy. You can share your values and be a leader to your kids and grandkids. You can share family stories and encourage the rest of the family to do the same, building a family lore everyone can identify with.

There's a long precedent for making the feeling of family a priority among dynasties who successfully transition wealth through generations. Mostly notably, the Rockefeller family, which has managed to keep its substantial wealth together for seven generations and counting, holds twice-yearly family retreats, often held at locations where the family has shared history and can experience the powerful feeling of legacy. Surprisingly, David Rockefeller, Jr., chairman of Rockefeller & Co., has gone on record explaining how the strength of his family brand is stronger for not having a shared business. The family, he explains, hasn't had a business-related dispute in over a century. The things they rally around—shared values, traditions, history, and philanthropy—are all uniting forces, not divisive ones.

In my experience, the primary goals families need to create the kind of culture that draws future generations closer are ensuring income security within the family, enlisting meaningful participation from all members, and creating an environment that fosters connection, integrity, purpose, and shared identity. Everyone has to have a seat at the table for it to work and to last. It takes a special family to create this kind of culture and avoid the loss of wealth, but it can be done.

CHAPTER 4

The Family Business: Sell It or Pass It On?

aking the right decision about whether and when to hold or sell can make a family rich over generations—or ensure its downfall. A family business that was started years or decades ago and built into a great asset is one of the most valuable investments in the world in its functioning form. It took years to build it, and if you are the founder, you undoubtedly think a lot about what to do with it. Should you sell it or keep it in the family? Maybe you have a trusted Number Two person who is not in the family, but you know that won't fly with your heirs. Maybe the outside person has been with you for years, but you can't see him or her taking ownership. Or you might have multiple children and step-children who can't take over or won't agree on how it should be done, and you can just imagine the strife ahead.

In order to keep your generous impulses from backfiring, you have to be able to look at your potential successors and be realistic. Is your son or daughter really capable of running the business? Does he or she want to? Can you imagine the two brothers or sisters you raised working peaceably together—or is that just a fantasy? If you want to see your legacy upheld and your wealth kept in the family, the worst mistake you can make is to pass on your business to an ill-prepared child and then have to watch it fall apart. In that scenario, no one is happy— not you, your spouse, your children, your grandchildren, or your employees. No one wins.

Your decision about the legacy of your business will be a key factor in keeping wealth in the family or condemning it to be lost. In my decades of working with business owners, I've seen it go bad far too many times. Doing this right is critical—one of the most important decisions you'll ever make. Let's look at the options in two scenarios.

In the first scenario, the family business is passed down with the idea of keeping the wealth together. In this case, it's an open secret within the family and the business that the son who will take over can't handle the job. Sure enough, the company slumps and continues to lose customers, reputation, and value until it eventually goes under. In this family—a real family, by the way—$50 million in assets go down the drain and with them any chance that any of the family wealth the owner/founder worked for decades to build would make it to the next generation. The biggest tragedy of all? Had he not grossly overestimated his son's ability to take over, the owner could have sold the business, preserved the family wealth, and ensured the son and the son's children would have stayed rich for decades.

A business owner has to have the honesty and guts to see the truth and call it like it is. If your children are flighty, irresponsible, greedy, lazy, or just not interested in running the kind of business you created, don't expect them to miraculously change.

In the second scenario, a family looks at the business and the heirs, at the strengths, weaknesses, and needs of both, and decides to sell. They get a fair price, creating immense liquid wealth in place of a functioning business that needs constant care and attention. Next, the wise family turns its attention to teaching the second generation and giving them the tools they need to respect, invest, and preserve the wealth they will inherit. Maybe they can have a fighting chance of getting it down to the third generation and beyond. Not everyone can be successful at this, but for many, getting the business out of the way is a step in the right direction.

While the majority of companies and families fare better when the business is sold, there are those that keep it together and do well. They tend to be exclusive territories or monopolies or oligopolies. If you are in a business where there is virtually no competition, it makes the decision harder. In those businesses (like distributorships with coveted territories, exclusive rights to a region, patented products, or brand name products of your own), you may have a real shot at the company being around for a long time.

One important caveat to all of this is that timing is critical. Don't let your sale window pass by while you sit around waiting for something bigger or better. If you hold out for an extra 5–6% and miss the sale of lifetime, you'll have to live with crushing regrets. Your industry, even if it's thriving today, may not be that special in 10 years. Think about the furniture business in the 1980s, fax/copier business before the internet, travel agencies, and dial-up services. Most businesses, even great ones, can be wiped out by competition or products that become obsolete or changed.

Luck plays a factor in selling at the right time and right place, but stubbornness and clinging to the past can get in the way even when fate is trying to give you a break. Xerox was top of the heap in 1975 only to lose out. Netflix put DVD companies almost out of business. Gillette didn't see Dollar Shave Club coming and it cost them. American Express doesn't own the payment market anymore. Investment guru Charlie Munger once said, "If you think you know what the state of the payments system will be ten years out, you're in a state of delusion."

Choosing to make carefully considered decisions about the future of your business while you are still at the top of your game is one of the most critical steps in maintaining family wealth. True to the psychology of staying rich, Gen-1 entrepreneurs know they must deal with their fears for the company themselves, rather than waiting for fate to sort them out.

PART TWO

If You Can Make It, You Can Lose It

CHAPTER 5

A New Place, A New Life

Many, if not most, first-generation wealth earners come from middle or lower socioeconomic classes. They've worked hard, often from childhood, scrapped, and scraped. When they make it, whether it's earning that first million dollars or selling a business for $10 million, $100 million, or more, they are a testament to the American dream.

The thing is, the journey to wealth is a psychological journey as well as a financial one. Even though these individuals acquire tremendous riches, for most their mindset is still tied to their upbringing. In my book *You Sold Your Company*, I classify business owners who've recently sold into four categories: leap frogs, butterflies, beavers, and lemmings. The leap frogs always want more. They grew up chasing and they always keep pushing; it's in their DNA. The butterflies were born well-off and developed out of a cocoon of wealth. They enjoy and appreciate what they have, and have a comfortable attitude toward being rich. The beavers seem saddled with their wealth, always hoarding it and never enjoying anything. And then there are the lemmings, who do what everyone else does, what they think is expected, and what they're told. Given the chance, they will easily, willingly march their wealth right over a cliff.

All of these former business owners must grapple with the subconscious needs and desires that helped drive their rise to wealth. The first step in the psychology of staying rich is knowing where your motivation lies and how to recognize—and when necessary deny—the deep-seated urges tied to that.

In my own case, I grew up extremely poor, living with the constant threat of having nothing. In my book *My Story*, I speak of having no money, no running water, of outdoor toilets, of hustling for work and paying my own way from the time I was just a kid. That kind of early relationship with money sticks with a person, and it creates problems. Even after I'd become financially successful, I still had my memories, and I still thought—too much—about what would happen if I lost everything. Fortunately, with reading and studying I was able to become secure, but the past still influences my decisions, just like it does yours.

Most business owners who sell come into their new lives, and their newly liquid wealth, with emotional baggage that impacts financial decisions for years to come—sometimes for the rest of their lives. I've seen hundreds of business owners who had enough wealth for a lifetime but could never be comfortable. They grew up with their backs to the wall, and that feeling remained their frame of reference. Sadly, too many of them proceeded to make rash, defensive decisions, leveraging too much or assuming too much risk—and ended up cornered again. Some people really do seem to subconsciously drag themselves back to where they feel they belong, no matter how much they have to lose to get there.

When these people come into new wealth, they often refuse to listen. They feel they have all the knowledge they need to handle wealth. After all, they made a lot more than anyone else, right?

What they don't know is that adapting to the new wealth must be learned through a different perspective than that of their middle-class roots. If you think about it, you've probably met some of the types we see most often: like the "we are just regular folks" who never acclimate because they don't want society to think they are uppity, or the "something to prove" crowd who go to all lengths to show off their wealth. Each group is a victim of its past. If you want to get ahead of the psychology of staying rich, start with your own history. What drove you to success? What bothers you about it? What worries keep you up at night?

How could the fears of your personal history haunt your invest-ing future? There are steps you can take that will help.

BE SELF-AWARE

Most first-generation wealthy people know that no matter how hard they worked to get what they have, luck also played a role. They know it intuitively—and if they think about it at all, they know bad luck can just as easily play a part in what happens to their fortunes.

Many people have a hard time adjusting to wealth—not just at first, but throughout their lives. Typically they go one of two ways: either they can't adjust because they feel guilty about leav-ing their roots behind, spending their time and energy trying to prove they haven't changed. Or they can't wait to show every-body they've *really* left their old lives behind. This second group spends a disproportionate amount of time doing things that say *Look at all this money.*

Neither of these approaches works. Rather than trying to prove something one way or the other, take the time to do some work on yourself. You've spent years, even decades, working on the business. Now work on your relationship with wealth, figuring out what you need to go through before you can be comfortable with what you have and the power it gives you.

I've known people who've had to do a little therapy work on always being afraid they're going to lose it all, but just acknowledging that your history plays a role in your present will help you gain some perspective. Start there and see where it leads you.

FIND MENTORS

If there's one thing your parents and old friends can't help you with as a first-generation wealth earner, it's learning how to get comfortable with being rich. Despite that, it does help to be able to follow in the footsteps of people who've gone before you and managed not to make a mess of their lives or their finances in the process. In my youth, I viewed people who had a leg up on me with a chip on my shoulder. As I became successful, I didn't think I needed help because I'd made it on my own. I was, like many self-made men, a renegade in my own mind. That attitude did me no good, and I had to learn that success in making money doesn't necessarily translate to success in keeping it or even in living well with it. I had to come to terms with the demons of growing up dirt poor, and I had to get comfortable with my financial security.

One thing that did help me—and a tool I've seen help many others—was seeking out people I admired for the way they'd adjusted to life with wealth. I'd ask for an hour of their time to hear about their experience, saying something like, *I'd like to ask you a few questions if you could spare the time.* When I did it, I got some incredible advice—advice it might have taken me a long while to figure out on my own. There's a reason people bid up the charity-auction lunch with Warren Buffet into the millions each year—and it's not that some fool thinks he or she will get rich with a couple hours' worth of advice. Those bidders are already rich. What they stand to gain, if they pay attention, is advice about investing for the long term, yes, but also about developing a healthy relationship with a mountain of money they have complicated feelings about.

If you're not 100% comfortable with your wealth, take the time to ask a few people you admire how they manage to be rich but also happy, grounded, and secure. Ask them how they got where they are, what mistakes they made, and what advice they have. You're not looking for tips on making more money; you're looking for an example of how to live in harmony with what you already have.

CHOOSE HONEST ADVISORS

Aligning yourself with advisors who will tell you straight when they think you're taking on too much risk or leveraging what should be bulletproof capital is a critical piece of hanging on to wealth. You need people you can trust to tell you when you're thinking with paranoia instead of strategy. We all need straight-talking individuals in our lives who are honest and direct, even if what they have to say sometimes isn't what we want to hear.

How can you identify the right folks for the job? For starters, they won't be trying to sell you the next big thing. They won't promise to exponentially grow your substantial wealth, overnight or ever. They won't *yes* you to death no matter how aggressive or risky an idea might be.

When you've already made your fortune, your wisest advisor is one who starts by telling you a portion of that wealth must be untouchable, locked away in low-risk investments—a tap you can turn on only if the world goes off the rails. This is your long-term security, and that money is hands-off for the foreseeable future. At Oxbow, we always advise separating this safety money from investment money. Once our investors do that, they've solved the problem of, *What happens if I go broke?*—because they won't. After that they can focus on other things— including higher-risk investments and growth opportunities. With their long-term security assured, they can afford to take a few chances in the here and now.

Pay close attention to the kind of financial advice you're getting. If it's all about chasing bigger and bigger returns without a focus on safeguarding your long-term security, you've got a problem that needs to be addressed before something catastrophic happens to your hard-earned wealth. If the answer is always, invariably, *yes,* you might start wondering if that's because your advising team doesn't have the wherewithal to say *No, and here's why.*

OXBOW NOTE

For a free copy of my book You Sold Your Company *and more about these theories and experiences, contact us at OxbowAdvisors.com.*

CHAPTER 6

The #1 Psychological Trait of Staying Rich

Over 40 years of working with wealthy individuals and families and watching how they operate, we at Oxbow have had plenty of time and experience to draw our own conclusions on what it takes to stay rich. Surprisingly, the key trait we see in those among this unique population who manage to hang on to their wealth is fear. It's the same fear that helped these people get rich in the first place. A fear of not having enough. A fear of losing what was hard gained. A fear of making a wrong choice or missing the right opportunity and contributing to a bad outcome.

This kind of deep-seated fear never really goes away, even in the face of success. It is powerful enough to keep the ego in check and keep you humble. It's a fear that comes with knowing there are no guarantees in life and that we are all continually playing the survival game. If you don't let it run your life, it can protect you, because people who live with this kind of fear tend to be observant of the fates of others—those who have invested recklessly, those who've had a hand in the government's bad business deals, and those who've been taken advantage of. People who live with fear are always thinking, always distrusting of security. That quality is so strong it seems nearly innate in everyone who accumulates wealth and keeps it.

So is this fear a burden? Is it too much to live with? Not really. Over time, it simply becomes a knowing, in the bottom of your gut, that you need to remain vigilant. That knowledge doesn't have to be a burden if you recognize it and make peace with it. It leads you to measure each investment closely for risk. It lets you recognize circumstances where the government is reaching for your wealth. It makes you wary of advisors who haven't proved themselves. When you owned a business, fear was what kept you on the lookout for what could go wrong. People who stay rich after they cash out carry that same feeling with them after the sale.

The pattern here is this: Getting rich is the biggest problem with staying rich. You get successful at something and become convinced you have it right. Then you get set in your ways and shut yourself off to change. If you aren't open to it, the always-changing world of investment will break you. If you want to be successful at staying rich, don't be so sure you already know everything. Let a little of that fear into your life. Nick Saban, the winningest coach in the history of college football, says he is always fearful—every game. He says he knows some small team could sneak up on him and beat his team if he loses his fear. That choice to never underestimate a challenge works equally well in the investment game.

Ask Polaroid or Eastman Kodak if they wished they had been fearful. Ask people who trusted Bernie Madoff to mind their money if they wished they had been fearful. Getting rich can make you feel bulletproof, but trust someone who has seen many of the mighty fall when I tell you that's only a feeling— not a fact.

AGE AND ATTITUDE PLAY A PART

Age can be a major factor in the fear trait, and it can work for you or against you. Generally, being a little older tends to make you cautious. If you sell a business at 50 years of age, you've likely seen enough bad deals to have learned a certain amount of fear, and that experience helps you.

At Oxbow we've seen many young people, 25–35 years old, sell businesses that make them a lot of money. Unfortunately, sometimes their success seems to have come too soon. Fearless and even arrogant, many of them lose their fortunes in a matter of just a few years. Most really believe they'll make it all over again, but the majority do not. They wake up one morning deciding they're going to become a developer, or partner in a start-up, or launch into an expensive business concept they know nothing about. They do it without caution, and they wipe out. These are the people who, when bad times come (and they always do), are too exposed. They're the ones who can't recover. Carrying some fear could have helped them stay stable and humble.

There's a fine line, though, between having the healthy fear that comes from experience and choosing to be complacent because of it. Tomorrow isn't going to be like yesterday in the investment world or anywhere else. Coming to liquid wealth with an attitude that says *I've always done it this way, and I'm not going to change* is setting yourself up for disaster. Think about how fast the world is changing. People who sold their businesses in the '90s are having to do things they never dreamed of today to stay relevant. They've moved on to laptops and cell phones and online businesses. There are a few who vowed to stay home with their landlines and not evolve, but they were left behind on a lot of levels long ago.

I'm not suggesting for even a minute that you should take your mountain of money and jump on every trend that comes your way, but at Oxbow we advise our investors to be open to new ideas—open to learning. Dick Clark, who managed to stay at the center of the music industry for decades, wrote that if he didn't try to understand new music and new artists, the music world would pass him by. That mentality— the desire to understand ideas that are new and different— is relevant in any industry and especially in taking care of your wealth. If you plan on doing anything different in your life once you've made your fortune, you have to keep up with changing times. Too cautious and your money doesn't work for you. Too aggressive and you're overexposed.

Your job in making the crossover to liquid wealth and staying rich is to be open to knowledge more than to change. Some of the coolest people I do business with are in their 80s, but they're texting and listening to podcasts and taking advantage of new technology. Listen and learn. Grow and change. Otherwise, your life was yesterday.

LOOKING DOWN THE ROAD

Most successful independent businesspeople carry a little fear. They know that things can happen. Even after they sell their companies and have sudden and vast liquid wealth, most keep at least a little of that edge. It can help insulate them against rash and overly risky investment choices (though of course it doesn't always). One worry almost all of these first-generation wealth earners face is knowing their children and their children's children don't have what they have. The kids are accustomed to absolute security—something the parents pride themselves on until one day they realize that having no experience with failure makes the kids vulnerable to being overconfident and quick to take chances. Gen-2 and Gen-3 are usually thinking about creating more wealth, when their first order of business should be making sure they keep what they have.

We make big jumps throughout our lives—high school to college, student to professional, beginner to boss in the business world, employee to entrepreneur. Of them all, the single biggest emotional jump anybody ever makes is suddenly coming into a lot of money after selling a company. If you've got that number one trait—a healthy fear of failure—you have a fighting chance to get that wealth down to the next generation and beyond.

OXBOW NOTE

If you recently sold your business, you're as vulnerable to wealth loss as you'll ever be in your life. For a free copy of my book Danger Time: The Two-Year Red Zone After Selling Your Company *and more books and videos on this subject, visit OxbowAdvisors.com.*

CHAPTER 7

Common Causes
of Wealth Loss

W hen we talk about the loss of giant sums of wealth, one response we hear a lot is, "Tell me it isn't true." Of all the things that are hard for the average investor to understand, nothing is more disturbing, confusing, and terrifying than the fact that someone could squander $20 million, $30 million, or even $100 million. There are over a million people in the US with net worth of $10–15 million, and over 150,000 with net worth over $25 million, but somehow we lose people from both of those groups each year. It never ceases to amaze me, but the story usually goes something like that of one family we dealt with in the late 2010s who sold their company for over $400 million. Over the course of less than three years, they lost more than half of it. It's possible to give good advice to even the most overconfident, bent-on-overspending, risk-loving investors, but it's not possible to make them take it. Once the spending floodgates open, some people are too egotistical and too proud to pull them back—and at that point there's little we can do for them.

On the other hand, I've worked with families who've sold for $20 million, $200 million, or even more who've made the crossover from running a business to managing a fortune with humble attention and caution. They've moved slowly, focused on maintaining, and worked not on making yet another fortune but on tending their family relationships and friendships. They don't spend their time trying to figure out what to *do* with all that money. They simply sleep well and have less worry in their lives because of it. It's a powerful feeling to know you can take care of you and yours for the rest of your lives, but for some people even that is never enough.

At Oxbow we've had a lot of time and opportunity to study the decisions that lead to losses of fortune, and there are a number of reasons we like to share in detail with those who are willing to listen and learn from our experience.

LOSS REASON #1: CONCENTRATION IN A SINGLE ASSET

Concentration in a single asset is a surefire way to put your capital at risk. If 80% or more of your wealth is in one stock, one real estate development, one start-up business, or any other single asset, that's a problem. Do any of these names ring a bell? Compaq, Kodak, Enron, Lucent, Tower Records, Polaroid, Pets.com, Worldcom? There are countless others on the list. I have been told more times than I can count by an investor who feels invincible after selling a public company that a particular investment is "going to the top," or that "there's no stopping it." They're completely confident, but after decades in the investment business, what I understand as fact is that even what appears to be a sure thing should never warrant investment of more than 20% of your assets. At that level, if the investment wins, you win. But if it fails, you live to play another day. So many people with newly liquid wealth feel their judgment is beyond reproach and live to regret their decisions.

LOSS REASON #2: THE INABILITY SAY NO

We all love our children and want them to be successful and happy, but families with wealth often try to buy success for their children instead of making them earn it. Many rich families get into the bad habit of endlessly funding lifestyle, business ventures, trips, and the like for children who then never learn to make it on their own. We'll talk more about this in later chapters, but over the years I've seen millions of dollars in family wealth go down the chute because parents could not say *No* to children who were losers and users.

LOSS REASON #3: LEVERAGE . . . THE KILLER BEE

So many people who have wealth forget that leverage is a tough adversary. It magnifies gains when things are going well, yes, but when things go poorly, it magnifies losses. If you have all the money you need for this lifetime and another, why leverage into another asset to get more? It may work—and it does at times—but the agony of defeat when things go wrong is devastating. A number of people I've known have taken their own lives because they couldn't live with the shame of having fallen so far from when they were on top of the world. Consider this: If you're already in possession of all the wealth you'll ever need, why not focus more on staying rich than on getting richer?

LOSS REASON #4: MISTAKING WEALTH FOR WISDOM

Being rich doesn't automatically make you a knowledgeable investor, but all too often that's exactly what newly wealthy people believe. People come into their money in all kinds of ways—and usually a combination of a few. Hard work is critical. Usually luck is, also. Intelligence matters. So does industry knowledge and understanding. But none of those things automatically makes you a wise investor—and they definitely don't give you the people smarts to recognize that there is a whole subculture of individuals and companies out there gunning for you and your money. They count on ego and ignorance combining to make you a soft target. It's the nature of business to humble those—even among the extremely rich—who get to feeling like big shots and misguidedly invest with questionable dealers who appeal to their pride instead of their good sense and intellect.

LOSS REASON #5: FAMILY DISCORD

This is a big one. Here is the picture: The first generation makes a fortune and life is good for the family. Then Mom and Dad die and the assets are left to the surviving children. This should be a smooth transition, but unless the parents spent considerable time preparing the kids—not the money—it rarely is. Instead, we often see the heirs go to war over the direction of the wealth, the sale of the business, or what a "fair share" is for each of them. Next steps: litigation, derailing the business, and outright stupid decisions based more in spite than in logic. This kind of discord among surviving family members destroys fortunes every day.

LOSS REASON #6: BEING ILL-PREPARED AND ILL-ADVISED

Managing significant financial assets is a skill set. None of us are born with it, and if you didn't grow up in a family that taught you how to manage money—not just an allowance but large sums and investments—you're probably not prepared for the job. People tend to believe that once they're rich, all their problems are solved, but money brings its own problems. If you are in possession of newly liquid wealth, do yourself a favor and find an experienced, trustworthy investment advisor with a proven track record and impeccable reputation to help educate and guide you in the care and keeping of your money.

There are many other reasons and ways people squander their riches: they spend too much; they're too trusting; they like to take risks. This isn't anything new. For as long as there's been money, fortunes have been made and lost, and in each generation countless families end up letting their wealth slip away and into someone else's hands. Part of it is just human nature, but if you go into it with the psychology of staying rich—if you're smart, careful, and humble—you can do a lot to guard against it.

OXBOW NOTE

First-generation wealth earners need to constantly guard against schemes designed to separate them from their wealth. These tests of your judgment don't always come in the form of shady characters with questionable reputations. Many show up polished, with the sheen of Wall Street on them. Just remember the caveat about buyer beware. If you'd like a free copy of Oxbow's analysis of the scams designed to separate you from your money, Wall Street Lies: 5 Myths to Keep Your Cash in Their Game, *contact us at OxbowAdvisors.com.*

CHAPTER 8

How the Long-Term Rich Invest

This chapter will undoubtedly draw criticism from the Wall Street crowd. I believe at Oxbow we have studied enough ultra-wealthy people to really understand how they stay rich. Most of them weren't told what to do; they just had enough fear and paranoia to end up ahead. All across the country, investment industry firms will show you every conceivable way to diversify, including many that you won't understand. Here's a simple fact: Most of the long-term rich investors we've seen concentrate their wealth in the same three primary areas of effective investment: income-producing real estate, private businesses, and semi-liquid equity like stocks, bonds, and cash.

Sure, there are endless possibilities out there, and we've seen great portfolios that include small but effective amounts of things like alternative energies, commodities, and collectibles, but the primary investments, by and large, stay to the three main lanes. Let's take a closer look at each.

LONG-TERM WEALTH STRATEGY #1: INCOME-PRODUCING REAL ESTATE

The rich have real estate. What type is the distinguishing factor between what gets passed to other generations and what does not. Investors that plow endless amounts of money into land or ranches don't necessarily make a mistake. It's just that their timing—selling and buying—needs to be perfect.

Here at Oxbow, we find that the vast majority of wealthy investors—90% or more—hold real estate as part of their wealth. Most of that is not mansions and islands and ranches, but in the form of income-producing property—multi-family housing, commercial property, industrial space, and retail space are the big four; with student housing and storage property coming in right behind.

Why is real estate key? It has all the ingredients to win the investment race. First, it has tax advantages that most investments can't touch. With depreciation, amortization, and, most of all, section 1031 exchanges, you could go your whole life and never pay capital gains taxes on your real estate investments. You only pay taxes on cash flow. Second, real estate has the added attraction of an inflation hedge, protecting you as the economy changes. Third, real estate is one of the easiest assets to get over to the next generation without costly consequences, as its valuation is subject to interpretation, unlike stocks and bonds that are quoted in the paper every day. Last, real estate is a physical, tangible asset in a world where many so-called investment opportunities are more conceptual than material.

LONG-TERM WEALTH STRATEGY #2: PRIVATE BUSINESS INVESTMENT

By private business we do not mean the Wall Street version of "private equity." Wall Street's private equity is, for the most part, a trumped-up idea by investment banks to lure money from investors. It is yet to be seen whether these funds will actually make money, but their investors have two significant factors working against them. The first is that these funds purchase all or pieces of companies at exorbitant prices. The second is that the funds are riddled with fees—acquisition fees, management fees, selling fees, etc . . . And there's another, potentially bigger problem any seasoned investor should recognize: He or she will never have a clean investment and will never have any say in the business.

Instead of Wall Street's private equity scheme, the real private businesses the rich can own and pass forward are direct ownership companies. These are investments in solid concepts, but equally important, in good people who can be trusted to see things through to long-term success. In this area, the long-term rich invest in the person, not just the deal. In addition to dealing with people you know and trust, this kind of investment also offers a simpler, more controlled approach. A 25% ownership investment, for example, equals 25% of the profits. It's a clean investment, simple and smart, and it lends itself to being passed from one generation to the next and keeping wealth in the family. If your private company investment does well, your family will be on the board, and your children will have a connection to and understanding of the business. They will feel and be invested for the long term.

LONG-TERM WEALTH STRATEGY #3: READY LIQUIDITY

The truly wealthy have always been diversified, but all participate in semi-liquid investments such as stocks and bonds. In the United States, studies have shown that the average ultra-high net worth person has 32–34% of their financial investments in cash. Having liquid and semi-liquid assets that can be on hand quickly provides the security of cash flow to use as you see fit—including having cash when everyone else seems to be out of it. In 2008–09, for example, when the real estate market was wrecked, cash-holding investors were able to buy at an advantage. People wonder why some among the wealthy stay that way, and one of the key factors is having liquidity when times are bad.

Part of the psychology of staying rich is sticking with what works and not chasing after every "hot," "exclusive," or "can't miss" investment opportunity that comes along. A wise advisor will help you choose a steady path that incorporates all three of these staples of long-term wealth.

PART THREE:

Next-Generation Failure — And How to Avoid It

CHAPTER 9

Keeping the Wealth Together

Most rich people have an inherent distrust of almost everyone outside the family. Wealthy siblings, in particular, often trust each other more than anyone else. They realize over time that far too many people want something from them because of their fortunes, but their siblings do not. When you get into third generations, cousins sometimes share this bond of trust, especially if the family fosters them having a shared sense of purpose.

One of the hallmarks of the psychology of staying rich is keeping the family—and by extension the family's wealth—together. There are a few approaches we at Oxbow have seen work reliably. Taking some (or all) of these steps together is often the most effective approach.

LET THE KIDS MAKE MISTAKES AND BE ACCOUNTABLE

If you want the next generations of your family to stay rich, treat them like they're not rich. That doesn't mean never spending money on them, but it does mean making sure they make their own decisions and are accountable. When your child or grandchild gets into a mess, don't come rushing to write a check to make things easier. Offer good advice if they ask, but don't offer an easy way out that is more about your wealth and power than their ability to solve a problem. Kids—and adults, for that matter—need consequences to learn. Kids learn by feeling and doing, not by watching Dad or Mom square things away for them.

MAKE SURE EACH GENERATION WORKS

Why work when your family has all the money you could ever need? Let's start with the basics. Work gives the individual a sense of purpose. Work builds self-esteem. Work teaches accountability. Work fosters the ability to get along with others. Work demands that the individual looks beyond his own needs to contribute to a greater goal. Can you think of any reason you wouldn't want your children and grandchildren to experience all these things? Everyone in the family needs to have the experience of working at a young age (not after 10 years of higher education or jet-setting) to become a fully realized individual.

Sometimes I hear from wealthy parents who say their kid can't get a job, and my response is, *make it happen*. In my own life I gave my friends with businesses cash to pay my children to work. My children weren't employees, but they thought they were. Most people won't hire a 12- or 13-year-old, but my friends and local business owners helped me out. My kids would come home and tell me their jobs were tough, and as a result they took a greater interest in education. Instead of roaming around town and hanging out at pool parties, they met their obligations at their jobs. In the long run, it made them more considerate, motivated, responsible adults.

GET OUTSIDE THE BUBBLE

Hand in hand with the requirement that your kids work should be the insistence that they do it outside the family. No good will come of raising future generations that are only answerable to you, and in my experience few things do more damage than raising a child to believe his or her fate is inevitably tied to the family business. Your kids may well become part of the family business one day. They may run the company or sit on the board. But if you want them to be successful at either of those things, they're going to need to want to do it and earn their place, not come to it thinking they were born to the role.

LOVE WITHOUT STRINGS

One of the surest ways to keep wealth together for future generations is sharing the values that the first generation had. How does a family go about doing that? Start by loving your kids and grandkids unconditionally. They may not think like you or act like you. They are unlikely to achieve like you have. They are going to have their own struggles and joys and achievements. One of the burdens of growing up in a wealthy family that rarely gets talked about is the expectation that the kids will be big achievers like the parents. Don't put that on your kids. Love them for who they are, and don't expect anything in return.

SHARE YOUR HISTORY

In far too many families, no one understands how the family wealth was amassed. The first generation may have worked seven days a week, always trying to make it. They may have had hard times, even broke times. They suffered, persevered, survived, and ultimately accumulated great wealth. Whatever their history, it's a critical part of the family's story and identity to share with the generations that follow—especially if you want to have any hope of preserving the family wealth.

The way to do this is by sharing your history and helping each member of the family feel like your story is their story too. Families that share strong histories, like those that share an immigration story or a past where religion plays a role or an experience that is especially tied to a particular place, foster strong bonds between all family members and the source of the family's wealth. The kids know their story. In families where land is involved, the tie is even more direct—if the kids get up every morning and work on the same farm or ranch as their parents and grandparents before them, then they experience the history of the business as their own. Whatever your story, as a member of Gen-1, you have a responsibility to build a strong family identity around it.

SET AN EXAMPLE

Future generations learn by watching their parents. They learn from seeing people who set a standard, not from those who talk about one. If the older generation spends no time with Gen-2 or Gen-3, what do they expect? If they sleep late, drink too much, have lousy marriages and crazy friends, and focus on money over family, they can expect the next generations to learn the same way of life. Show your kids the values that matter to you through your actions, and they'll be more likely to take them to heart.

SHARE A PURPOSE

One of the key ways to keep both family and family wealth together is through philanthropy. All generations can partici-pate in philanthropic endeavors, and those endeavors benefit both the family and society. Even after a family business is gone, a family philanthropy can live on and give the next generations a shared purpose. Charitable foundations can be an especially effective way to help Gen-3 and Gen-4 to successfully participate in the family and in its wealth.

HARNESS THE POWER OF TRUSTS

The farther removed a generation is from the person who created the wealth, the harder it is to keep it together. In some families, Gen-3 individuals may not know the first generation at all. Because of this, one of the biggest challenges in keeping family wealth together is posed by the number of heirs. Gen-2 or 3 may make millions of dollars on a deal, but that might not move the needle on the family wealth. In Gen-1, a million made from scratch was momentous. For next generations, it may not mean as much. One of the only ways to ensure available wealth for future generations is through trusts, and almost all families who are successful in keeping their wealth together over generations use them. Trusts sometimes get a bad reputation for being too controlling, but there are ways to construct them so they're a powerful tool in the heirs' hands, not a leash on them. For many high-net-worth families, there's simply too much on the line not to use this effective wealth-management tool.

OXBOW NOTE

Why not write a small book for your heirs that chronicles your life and times and at the same time cautions family members against wasting family wealth? I wrote one myself and gave my children a new perspective on the struggles, sacrifices, and accomplishments of my life. At Oxbow Advisors (oxbowadvisors.com), we can help you document your story and get it printed for your family.

CHAPTER 10

Generation Gap

An estimated 80% of all wealth is made in the first generation. Think about that for a moment. It means that through time, only 20% of wealth stays with the family. Where is the hang-up in this critical transfer? It typically starts the minute the second generation takes a role. Why? Because the first generation made the money. They honed their instincts for business and for survival. Most were financially conservative—watching spending, investing wisely, and preserving capital. Gen-2, Gen-3, and beyond did not have the opportunity to develop this skill set. So if you want them to become good wealth managers and stewards of the family legacy, you're going to have to teach them.

The ability to guide your child to being accomplished, responsible, and fulfilled is a big job, but it's one with a more satisfying outcome than any other endeavor. Among the percentage of Gen-2 from wealthy families who do well, most have been taught to have a strong work ethic and to live full and normal lives. Many of them go on to be as good or better business-people than Gen-1 because they had excellent mentoring and training from their parents.

First, let's talk about the 80%—the Gen-2 heirs who let the hard-earned fortunes of their families slip through their fingers like so much sand. In 40 years of watching business owners build companies, create wealth, and try to keep it in their families, I've seen countless ways for the heirs to blow it all up. Some are clueless, confidently making costly, rash decisions until the money's gone. Some are nearly worthless, wasting their days with hanger-on friends, parties, trips, and drugs. Many just aren't prepared to handle wealth, and so they entrust it to unworthy investment guides, advisors, and friends with "can't lose" investments that almost always fail.

What should you do if you are the Gen-1 money maker? First of all, teach responsibility. You can't teach that if you put a new BMW in your kid's hands at 15. You can't teach it if they sleep in every morning and stay out all night, or if they have no understanding of philanthropy and the rewards that come from helping others. And you can't teach it if they get to be 18 and have never had a job. I believe the most danger-ous words ever spoken by people who've made great fortunes are, "I want my kids to have it easier than I did." If you want to see the ugly side of wealth, track down a few of those parents a decade or two later and ask them how that's working out. Rich parents have to put in the work just like parents from every socioeconomic class, and if you're wise you'll start teaching your kids today—no matter what their age—that the psychology of staying rich starts with becoming and remaining a productive member of society.

HANDS-ON EXPERIENCE

If you really want your children to be able to step up and manage the family wealth one day, they need hands-on experience while you're still able to offer some support and guidance. There is no point in forcing this experience onto members of Gen-2 or Gen-3 who aren't interested in learning, but for those who are, a method that works really well centers around a piece of income- producing real estate. This is both a sturdy investment and an excellent teaching tool.

The young investor should take point in finding the property, building a business plan with balance sheets and income statements, then going to the bank to set up financing. He or she should be the person who shakes hands, looks the banker in the eye, and sits across the table throughout the process. You can agree to loan the down-payment or sign for the loan as long as Gen-2 runs the property. This means capital expenditures, leases, insurance, taxes, and maintenance.

Over the course of a number of years, your next-gen participant will likely see the property increase in value, see cash flows going up, and realize real estate is not a bad investment. He or she will learn something practical and immediate that will stick.

Another way first-generation wealth earners can have the same positive, proactive impact on their heirs is by walking alongside them as they try their hand in business. If the Gen-2 individual comes to you with a well-thought-out business plan (five years with reasonably projected profitability), help them secure financing. This is very different from buying a business *for* the child. Instead, it's about standing beside them as they figure out a way to finance, acquire property and insurance, hire, operate, and eventually pay the bank back. Throughout all those steps, the learning is happening—not just in terms of financial world realities, but also in terms of what it's like for the person to invest his or her own effort. Whether the business does well and the heir makes it and feels good about it, or the business doesn't do well and it hurts them, they will learn more through this process than they could ever learn by just thinking and talking about wealth management. This business isn't a gift, but it is an education.

Contrast either of these approaches with having this same heir go see a financial advisor who throws Wall Street terms around for a couple hours, causing their eyes to glaze over and them to continue to think about wealth in hypothetical terms. Which makes more sense to you?

THE SHORT TERM MATTERS

Without some kind of in-depth experience, everything your heirs think they know about investing will probably boil down to *we buy stocks, markets go up and down, we make or lose money.* This is a problem. Regardless of how much money the family has, the heirs need to learn that short-term losses do matter. When some Wall Street salesman tells them not to worry about the short run, they need to walk away. There are basic financial tenets that the people who will keep your wealth in the family need to understand, and that's not one of them. Teach your family about good debt (which cash flow can easily cover) and bad debt, about term life to cover all debt, about keeping plenty of liquidity for two to three years of living expenses at all times, about spending less than they make, about not taking any risk that could potentially put them under. These are the lessons every person who's going to inherit substantial family wealth needs to learn—not some flippant *there's more where that came from* mentality.

More and more, we're seeing this idea, born on Wall Street and taking root across the country, of taking the kids to a "wealth advisor" (which is a terrible term that ignores the fact most of these people don't have any wealth themselves) and letting that individual teach the children how the investment world works. All I can say about that whole dynamic is, *Don't.* Real-world stuff does not go on in the "wealth advisor's" office. It goes on in transactions, in the nuts and bolts of business.

WHO PAYS THE RENT?

One last critical tenet of families that manage to get money down from generation to generation is that the senior generations don't let their wealth go toward living expenses for the younger. They are not a piggy bank, while they're alive or after they're gone. They may fund educations; they may partner in businesses; they may offer job opportunities and other kinds of advantages—but they don't just cut monthly checks.

The world doesn't work on an allowance, and the sooner your offspring understand this, the better. They need to figure out how to depend on *work* rather than just on *money*. When they rely on themselves, they will also learn to be confident, independent thinkers. If you have the ability to allow your next generation to stand on their own two feet, you will have given them the greatest gift in the world. The irony of it is that if you succeed in this, you'll have made great strides in preparing your heirs to eventually inherit and preserve your wealth.

CHAPTER 11

Individuals Are Assets

Many wealthy families benchmark their success in strictly monetary terms. They tally their assets, count their money, and track their investments. They spend much of their time on the correct placement of their money. Too often, they gauge family wellness on wealth.

What these families fail to realize is that wealth is only one of the legs that allows families to stand, financially secure, for generations. If you study families that have stayed rich over time like we have at Oxbow, you discover that they place equal importance on a second priority: the heirs themselves. Families with both wealth and wisdom understand that their children and grandchildren are their most important family assets. What's more, they know that investing in these human assets requires much more than just setting up trust funds and ensuring financial support. People are just people regardless of wealth, and we all need to feel wanted, we all need to live with a sense of purpose, and we all need to achieve and accomplish goals in our own right to thrive and be happy. It is a critical part of the psychology of staying rich that the earning generation recognizes this fact to be true for every generation that comes after them.

How does a rich family recognize and help meet these needs in its children and grandchildren? Start by helping them learn to survive on their own. Encourage them to find educational and professional purpose. Insist that their lives be about more than who they are, focusing instead on what they do. And show them by your example that wealth is just a small part of what defines your quality and character.

When my own kids went off to college, I told them to do what they love and become the people they wanted to be. Be a plumber. Be a doctor. Go for it and figure yourself out. Know that you have a parent who loves you under any circumstance. You're on your own, but you're not alone.

Consider these two families, based on hundreds of real families I've worked with over the years. Both were founded by smart, hard-working entrepreneurs. Both created first-generation wealth of over $100 million. Both sold businesses to acquire that massive amount of money.

That is the end of the similarities between them.

The first family is one I call the F Family, because they failed miserably to hold on to their wealth and managed to raise unhappy heirs in the process. With $100 million in assets to begin the next phase of their lives after selling a business, they concentrated almost exclusively on the financial aspect of their futures and neglected the rest. They worked to ensure their children had and would continue to have wealth, but they didn't bother to guide them toward being self-supporting, contributing adults. The kids never had to get or hold jobs, never learned to build meaningful relationships in which their family wealth didn't matter, never found livelihoods that helped them feel fulfilled. They were spoiled and shallow, disrespectful of the hired help who made their lives easier, and surrounded by so-called friends who hung around for the perks of being connected with the money. To them wealth was just a fact of life, one that bought them whatever they needed, including the smoke screen of positions that looked like careers and the attention of anyone in their orbit who might be able to sell them something or otherwise take advantage of their position.

Where were the parents who made the F Family's fortune in this scenario? They were congratulating themselves on setting their children and grandchildren up for life. *We gave them enough to last a lifetime* was their mantra. They also set an appalling example of constant, mindless consumption. They thought their work was done, and in accepting that they set an entropy in motion in the next generation that would eventually wipe out the family's wealth. Their legacy is one of materialism and disrespect and waste.

Let me tell you, the downfall of a family like this is painful to watch as it unfolds. Fortunately, it doesn't have to be that way. There are families who manage to not only preserve their wealth, but also to help ensure that second leg—the individuals in subsequent generations—are secure and thriving. Let's talk about one of those families, one I call the A Family because of their extraordinary success in understanding that money is only a single aspect of family wealth.

The A Family also had $100 million in earned wealth, but they handled it completely differently. The first generation worked incredibly hard to earn this money, but they also made sure their children worked hard. As their net worth grew, most aspects of their lives didn't change much. They certainly didn't lavish money on their kids. Instead, as parents they stayed focused not on what the kids *had*, but on what they *did*. They taught the next generation through their example to measure themselves and others by their contributions to society and by the way they treated people.

As the kids in the A Family reached adulthood, they took mortgages. They borrowed money if they wanted to start businesses. They lived below their means and saved. They turned to their parents not for handouts, but for advice on making good investments and business decisions. Even though the family's wealth was there to give them safe harbor if they needed it, these young adults made their own way, built their self-esteem, and learned to appreciate the value of wealth. As time passed, they eventually learned about sound financial strategies and the family investments from their parents and their trusted advisors. This family invested as much of its energy and time in its children's personal successes as it did in its financial interests, and both were successful.

This is the way a family hangs on to its wealth from generation to generation—by remembering the money is only a small piece of who they are. If you do this right, then your wealth doesn't become the thing your kids define themselves by, and it doesn't become the source of their daily income. It becomes a backstop. A safety hatch. A measure of security that lets them have the privilege of knowing that even if the world goes to hell tomorrow, they will be okay.

In their 2004 book *Hats Off to You*, authors Ernest Doud and Lee Hausner wrote about the father and founder of a successful business whose son worked there. The son, overconfident and underachieving, thought he was above reproach but was seen as incompetent by the other employees. When a major position opened up in the company, the father met the son for lunch. The son, thinking the job was his for the taking, arrived to find two hats on the table, one that said BOSS and one that said DAD. The father put on the BOSS hat and said, "Son, you're fired." Then he put on the DAD hat and said, "Son, your mother and I are deeply concerned that you are unemployed. How can we help you?"

The A Family understood, like Doud and Hausner's dad/boss, that ensuring kids have the know-how to stay rich is just as important as providing them with the money.

All too often, the individuals are the overlooked assets in the psychology of staying rich, but the fact is, you can estate plan and tax plan for years on end and still be a failure at passing down wealth if you don't give this component of your legacy equal attention. How your heirs understand the world, their place in it, and the role of wealth in their lives is critically important. Without strong values and experiences in this area, they'll be destined to blow your so-called dynasty.

OXBOW NOTE

For more on the subject of raising families who aren't tainted by wealth, you can request a free copy of my book Rich Kids, Broke Kids: The Failure of Traditional Estate Planning *at Oxbowadvisors.com.*

CHAPTER 12

You Need to Talk about Money

Many of us in the earning generation grew up without money and were taught all our lives that talking about it was socially verboten, even within the family. As a consequence, many wealth creators plan every aspect of their children's financial lives through advisors, leaving the heirs out of the conversation altogether. This is a big mistake.

There's a conversation every worthy investment advisor should have with every wealthy client, but very few bother because it is emotional and uncomfortable. Ironically, it's about an emotional and uncomfortable conversation you owe it to your family to have with your kids. So let's get started.

If you had a heart attack tomorrow and became incapacitated or died, life would change, instantly and forever, for your spouse, your children, and the people who depend on you for their livelihood. Would your family know what to do? Would they know how to take care of you, your estate, your assets? Would they be prepared to take care of each other? Would they understand the responsibilities of managing wealth and be ready to assume them? Would they know who to turn to for guidance?

If you can't answer each of these questions with a humble, confident *Yes*, you are failing your family and failing one of the biggest tests of psychological preparedness for staying rich. If you don't want to talk about it or think about it, get over that. If you're keeping secrets, waiting to drop a bombshell when your will is read, stop it now. If you're overwhelmed with the complexity that would be involved in a worst-case plan, then ask yourself: How impossible would it be for your spouse or heirs to create one without your guidance?

Weak and short-sighted people avoid these conversations, but those with both wealth and wisdom know talking about money is critical, so they make it happen.

This is a complex matter, one that can't be settled in a single conversation, but the sooner you get started, the better. If you don't have any idea where to start, the best place is with your spouse. Sit down together and set guidelines regarding what you are going to leave your heirs, when you will give it, and whether that transfer will be via trusts, gifts, or some other vehicle. Talk about whether you are going to treat your children equally, and if not, why not? When are you going to tell them and what do you want to say? You should have clear, agreed-upon intentions between the two of you before you ever get around to talking with the heirs.

While you and your spouse work though the details, there are a lot of other intricacies to consider. Following is a list of primary concerns. If you aren't sure how to tackle this whole process, you can enlist trusted legal and/or financial advisors to help you. At Oxbow, this is an area where we have a lot of experience making sure the important issues are addressed:

- Do your children know about your wealth—where it comes from, how it is held, how it is managed?

- Have you explained your financial philosophy to your heirs—the choices you've made and why? The choices you hope they'll one day keep in mind as they make their own?

- Do your heirs understand the size of your estate and the options that might be available to them, including real estate, private business investment, and equities? Do they know about insurance, savings, and debt aversion?

- Does your family understand your wishes for end-of-life care?

- Do your children know who you trust in the world of financial advising and why?

It doesn't matter if you think your situation is too complicated or messy or if you think your kids don't care. These are necessary conversations that almost universally put families on the path to better long-term wealth outcomes.

The wealth-creating generation has a responsibility to teach financial discipline, independence, humility, and the roles money should—and should not—play in daily living. Here at Oxbow we have seen the sad results of wealthy business owners keeping everything from the children instead of having frank conversations about money.

There are tools to help facilitate this process that you may not have considered, and there are also tools for helping your family understand how and why your wealth-management philosophy came to be. Sometimes understanding the origins of principles can help make them more relatable to the heirs. Share your story with your kids. In my own life, I took the time to write a book about my experience, laying out how my career and wealth happened, the origins of my values, and my hopes for my family's future. I recommend this process or something similar for anybody who is struggling with how or what to say to their kids. The Oxbow staff can arrange help for you in writing your story or creating a family history video, or you can do these things on your own. Either way, creating an enduring record can serve as a jumping-off point for discussions you need to be having with your family. Rich kids, just like any other kids, need to be taught. Leaving them to simply figure out how to handle your legacy on their own is a recipe for disaster.

If you've made a fortune, you owe it to yourself to accept the burden of sharing the basic knowledge and essential psychology of staying rich with the next generation in your family. Get started while you still have time.

OXBOW NOTE

Because this is such a critical issue to wealth preservation, at Oxbow we excel not just in helping families with money but in structuring arrangements so that money doesn't disappear in the next generation. For more information about how to approach legacy planning in your own family, contact us at OxbowAdvisors.com.

What Matters Most

M oney alone can only go so far. It can make some aspects of life easier, giving you choices and a measure of safety. But in reality, most of the security money provides is all in your head. No amount of wealth can negate the fact that we are all still just fragile humans, and death, sickness, mental challenges, and family and business problems can come into our lives at any time. Maybe that's why most of the high-net-worth investors we at Oxbow ask about their priorities don't talk about beating the indexes, avoiding taxes, or even getting the best return on their investments. Instead, they want to know how they can ensure the wealth they've earned will take care of their loved ones. Our investors want to know how to provide security for children and grandchildren, how to ensure the legacy of their wealth isn't fighting within the family, how to make wise and fair decisions whether they're dealing with smart and high-achieving offspring or those who are struggling or not even self-sufficient. When it comes down to it, the heart of their concerns is family over portfolio, every time.

Almost every wealthy family we deal with wants to help its heirs build wealth and success. We all know there's no such thing as guaranteed safety for future generations, but we encounter many investors who have reached the age where they're not focused on making the next million dollars anymore so much as they're thinking, "How much time can I spend with my spouse, children, and grandchildren?" and "How can I help ensure the people I love will be okay when I'm gone?" As we get older, we encounter more and more people who had everything and lost it—not just money, but wellness and peace in the family. Most of us have been on the receiving end of a phone call that a close friend or relative—a peer, not some old timer—died suddenly. And we've thought, *That could have been me.* We attend memorials and look around and ask ourselves what we have done to prepare our families, and our fortunes, for the long term. It is in the fourth quarter of life that the wise and the wealthy lock in on new priorities: legacy, philanthropy, and most of all, family. Maybe that focus is one of the most important pieces of the psychology of staying rich. It's not about how much wealth you have. It's about how you're going to use that wealth to foster long-term security, peaceful partnerships, and an enduring legacy among the people who matter to you.

We hope this book about the psychology of staying rich has given you new insight into the qualities and plans of families who stay rich for generations. So many families fail at this ultimate test of accomplishment. With determination and attention to detail, you can ensure your family's long-term financial security and their pride in being a part of your legacy.

OxbowAdvisors.com
512-386-1088